THE NATIONAL TRUST

Desk Diary

2000

THE NATIONAL TRUST

Published in Great Britain in 1999
The National Trust (Enterprises) Ltd, 36 Queen Anne's Gate
London SW1H 9AS

© 1999 The National Trust

Registered Charity no. 205846

ISBN 0 7078 0315 2

FRONT COVER: Scobbiscombe Farm, near Kingston on
the south coast of Devon. (*NTPL/David Noton*)

BACK COVER: A Dutch mastiff, probably called Old Vertue, in a late
seventeenth-century painting by Jan Wyck. The artist has depicted the
house at Dunham Massey in Cheshire on the left, and the dog gambolling
amongst the sheep on the estate on the right. (*NTPL/John Hammond*)

Articles by Margaret Willes, Publisher, The National Trust

Picture Research by Margaret Willes and Sophie Blair

Designed by Humphrey Stone

Astronomical information reproduced, with permission from data,
produced by HM Nautical Almanac Office
© Particles Physics and Astronomy Research Council

Phototypeset in Monotype Sabon Series 669
by SPAN Graphics Ltd, Crawley, West Sussex (SG1570)

Printed by Tien Wah Press Ltd, Singapore

Introduction

The arrival of the year 2000 is inevitably portentous. Some people may say that it does not mark the millennium, which should be observed in 2001. But our ancestors certainly did not think that – when the year 1000 came up, many predicted the end of the world or the Second Coming. So I am taking this to be the diary for the millennium, and have chosen an appropriate theme – time – and applied it to landscapes.

When W. G. Hoskins wrote the foreword to a new edition of his *Making of the English Landscape* in 1977, he declared in bold type, 'Everything is older than we think'. He was talking about the developing role that archaeology had played in landscape interpretation in the twenty years since his ground-breaking book first appeared. But he was absolutely right: peel back the layers of a landscape like an onion, and more layers are revealed underneath. Those layers can be physical, as in geology or archaeology, or less tangible, as in climatology or cultural history.

I have tried to make my choice of landscapes as regionally diverse as possible, and to take a different approach to each. When looking at the Giant's Causeway, for example, I have concentrated on the geological debate and the development of tourism, for Avebury on its long history as a site of religious significance, for the White Cliffs of Dover on their role as a place of refuge and of defence.

The National Trust is celebrating the millennium by focussing on the Neptune Coastline Campaign, which was launched to protect the coastline of England, Wales and Northern Ireland. Those of us who live in these countries are never more than seventy miles from the sea, and somehow this fact has entered our souls and our affections, for Enterprise Neptune (as it was formerly called) has proved very successful in its thirty-five years of existence. But it has more work to do because, as I show in this diary, the coast is very vulnerable. I am very grateful to Richard Offen, Neptune's Appeal Manager, and his assistant Hilary Moorcroft, for their enthusiasm and for persuading me to include so many coastal landscapes.

Because study of the landscape crosses many disciplines, I have depended on a whole host of people to help me. In particular, I am grateful to the following: Steve Judd, Adrian Colston, Chris Gingell, Jon Brookes, Paul Boland, Peter Katic, Jonathan Fisher, Dennis Rooney, Angus Wainwright, Mary Salter, David Adshead, David Thackray and Rob Woodside; and there are no doubt others whom I have omitted. My thanks to you all.

Margaret Willes, Publisher, 1999

The White Cliffs of Dover: The Front Line

The chalk cliffs of Dover represent one of the symbolic landscapes of Britain. Here the North Downs run into the English Channel, the cliffs formed from the fossil remains of myriads of microscopic sea creatures which settled at the bottom of the ocean over 100 million years ago. In sunlight the cliffs are a brilliant white – sharp-eyed Romans, looking out from the shores of Gaul, noted them and called the mysterious island Albion from *alba*, the Latin for white. When shrouded in misty rain they can look a wan grey, while sunrise and sunset imbue them with a golden glow.

This south east corner of Kent is only twenty miles away from the French coast, the narrowest point between the British Isles and mainland Europe. It is thus both a place of refuge and of threat. For returning travellers, the white cliffs were a sign that they were home – providing they could cope with the notorious shoals and banks of the Goodwin Sands which were dubbed 'the Great Ship Swallower'. For those who came to conquer, they represented Britain's first line of defence.

This combination of refuge and defence can be clearly seen at Dover Castle, now looked after by English Heritage. On the highest point of the site of an Iron Age fort the Romans built a lighthouse or *pharos*, with an answering light to the west on what is now Drop Redoubt. Octagonal towers with stepped stages rising to 80 feet in height were surmounted by braziers, lit to guide sailors into the harbour in between. Four stages of the Dover Castle lighthouse survive next to the church of St Mary in Castro, founded in AD 1000.

Visitors to Dover Castle are provided with a varied menu of history reflecting the key role it has played in the defence of the realm over the centuries. William the Conqueror built the first castle here soon after his victory at Hastings in 1066, and it was garrisoned right through to 1958. Sometimes Dover's impregnability proved a close run thing. In 1216 French troops under Prince Louis invaded and laid siege to the fortifications. To counter this, tunnels were constructed to enable English soldiers to make their way to the northern outworks, and to gather for attack.

When Napoleon threatened to invade nearly 600 years later, more tunnels were dug through the yielding chalk, and these came into use again in 1940 when Dover became the headquarters of Admiral Bertram Ramsay as he directed Operation Dynamo, the evacuation of over 338,000 Allied soldiers from the beaches of

Dishing out food in the Royal Army Medical Corps dressing station in one of the underground tunnels below Dover Castle during World War II. (English Heritage Photographic Library)

Dunkirk. While the Battle of Britain was fought in the skies overhead, and supply convoys struggled through the Channel, Dover was provisioned to withstand a six-week siege in the event of the expected German invasion. Although this never took place, Dover and the adjacent coast remained in range of German artillery set up on the French coast, and this part of Kent became known as Hellfire Corner. The tunnels have been reopened and provide an atmospheric setting for a dramatic retelling of this extraordinary story.

After all these alarums and excursions, the five miles of coast owned by the National Trust stretching east around Langdon Cliffs to St Margaret's Bay provide a haven of peace and natural beauty. Vera Lynn got it romantically wrong when she sang of bluebirds flying over the white cliffs of Dover. Shakespeare was nearer the mark in *King Lear* when Edgar describes the cliff edge to his blinded father, the Earl of Gloucester:

> How fearful
> And dizzy 'tis to cast one's eyes so low!
> The crows, and choughs that wing the midway air,
> Show scarce so gross as beetles: Halfway down
> Hangs one that gathers samphire; dreadful trade!

The chalk grassland provides a habitat for a wide range of flora and fauna. Lesser Black-backed Gulls, Fulmars, Rock Pipits and the only breeding colony of Kitti-wakes in Kent make their homes here, while the cliffs are a vital point of arrival and departure for migrant birds. Flowers include Horseshoe Vetch, Meadow Clary and several varieties of orchid, including Pyramidal and Bee. These are encouraged by grazing Exmoor ponies and sheep on the grassland to keep the coarser grasses down. There are lots of butterflies, including Chalkhill Blue and Adonis Blue. This area is also a natural vegetable patch, with Wild Thyme, Wild Carrots and Alexanders, and 'poor man's asparagus', the Samphire mentioned by Shakespeare.

The National Trust is improving its provision for visitors on Langdon Cliffs by building a low, mainly wooden structure with a turf roof to blend in with the surroundings. Acknowledging the generosity of its major sponsor, it will be called the Saga Gateway to the White Cliffs and provide not only visitor facilities but also space for exhibitions and a wonderful seaward view of the constant activity in Dover harbour.

Walkers making their way under the cliffs come across heavy gun sites and caverns used for 'fighting lights' to track down German planes and boats during the Second World War. By the shore they see the wreck of the *Preussan*, a sailing ship that ran aground in 1910. At South Foreland they come to the lighthouse that was erected in 1843 to help sailors navigate the Goodwin Sands. Originally lit by oil, it later became the first electrically powered light in the British Isles. Once out of sight of land, however, ships were still entirely isolated until Marconi, using radio transmission, carried out the first ship-to-shore demonstration from South Foreland to the East Goodwin lightship, a distance of twelve miles. This took place in foul weather over Christmas and New Year 1898, celebrated by Marconi's devoted assistant, G. S. Kemp, with a prolonged bout of seasickness on board the lightship.

Yet another first for South Foreland will be the dawn of the millennium. It has been predicted that the sun will strike the lighthouse at 7.56am on 1 January 2000, the first place to see daylight in Britain.

The Giant's Causeway: A Place Worth Seeing

The Giant's Causeway is one of the most spectacular features of the Antrim coast in Northern Ireland. It was formed 60 million years ago when volcanic activity caused the earlier chalk landscape to be covered by layers of lava. This surface began to weather, creating a layer of soil, which now shows as a red seam. On top came another layer of lava which lost its heat slowly and evenly, creating regular cracks like drying mud, and cracking vertically too, to produce polygonal columns that now look so strange and man-made. In all there are 40,000 of these columns on the Irish coast, with a similar formation on the Scottish island of Staffa.

This is the geological explanation, but of course legends have grown up to explain the phenomenon. Perhaps the most famous involves two giants: on the Irish side, Finn MacCool, with his wife Oonagh and his baby son, Oisin; on the Scottish side, Benandonner. Finn was visiting the north coast bay of Port Noffer (Gaelic for Bay of the Giant) when he learnt that Benandonner was threatening to capture his lands. To sort out Benandonner, Finn built the Giant's Causeway across to Staffa by collecting rocks and carving them into columns. But on arrival in Scotland, and seeing the size of his adversary, he thought better of his adventure and beat a hasty retreat, kicking off a boot on his way, still to be seen at Port Noffer. Benandonner, catching a brief glimpse of Finn, took off after him, pursuing him to his very door. Oonagh promptly dressed Finn in his baby son's bonnet, wrapped him in blankets, and put him in the cradle with a dummy to suck. When Benandonner saw the size of the baby, he realised that Finn must be huge, so returned to Scotland, tearing up the causeway as he went. Fingal's Cave on Staffa, celebrated by Mendelssohn in his *Hebridean Overture*, recalls this encounter.

Although inhabited since prehistoric times, the Causeway was unknown to the rest of the world, making its appearance on the map of Ireland only in 1714. It was the Royal Society, incorporated by Charles II to meet and discuss 'new or experimental philosophy', that brought the Giant's Causeway to the eyes of the world. In 1694 Dr Samuel Foley, Bishop of Down and Connor, wrote a paper for the Society that included a drawing showing a series of rounded hillocks rather than the columnar rocks. But he instituted a scientific debate about it which was to run for nearly a century, and seemed particularly to appeal to churchmen.

The protagonists divided themselves into the Neptunists and the Vulcanists. The Neptunists believed that the phenomenon of the Causeway was the result of particles in the sea water settling on the sea-bed and becoming first mud, then columns. The Vulcanists plumped for a volcanic origin. In 1740 Susanna Drury, a little-known artist from Dublin, spent three months on site to produce two paintings that were then made into engravings and distributed throughout Europe. They provided at last a good understanding of the stones, but confused as well as informed. Some Vulcanists put her prospects side by side so that they created a mountain in the middle, and thus deduced that lava had flowed from it. Frederick Hervey, 4th Earl of Bristol and Bishop of Derry, combined an interest in geology with a passion for travel – the Hotels Bristol still to be found in Europe are testament to the latter. In 1770 he wrote to his nephew, 'You have doubtless heard much of our Giant's Causeway. Till lately it has been reckon'd single of its kind but I have lately discovered such varieties of the same sort both in France and Italy, and accompanied with such peculiarities of soil as can no longer leave the origin of the strange phenomenon a Problem.' The Problem was about to be solved by a fellow churchman, Dr William Hamilton, Rector of Clondevadock in Donegal. He concluded correctly that the Causeway was part of a larger volcanic area, publishing his findings in *Letters Concerning the Northern Coast* in 1786.

By this time the Giant's Causeway was attracting tourists from all over Europe. A road had been built down to the stones of the Causeway in the late seventeenth century, but it was frequently impassable and visitors had therefore to leave their carriages on the clifftop and make their way down on foot, or approach by boat. The novelist William Makepeace Thackeray paid a visit in 1842 and his woes could be echoed by many a visitor to popular tourist sites today: 'Mon Dieu, and have I travelled 150 miles to see that! The guides pounce upon the visitor, with a dozen rough boatmen who are lying in wait … I had no friends: I was perfectly helpless … Four men seized a boat, pushed it into the water, and ravished me into it.'

Local women sitting in the
Wishing Chair on the
Causeway; a photograph
taken in the late nineteenth
century. (Ulster Museum)

Local women sitting in the Wishing Chair on the Causeway; a photograph taken in the late nineteenth century. (Ulster Museum)

Local inhabitants combined fishing and burning seaweed, to provide kelp for soda and iodine, with duties as guides and sellers of fossils and crystals. Thackeray describes one such, Old Mary, who sold whiskey and water from a wishing well on the Little Causeway. 'Did you serve Old Saturn with a glass when he lay along the Causeway here?' he asked. 'In reply she says she has no change for a shilling; she never has: but her whisky is good.'

In 1855 the Belfast to Portrush railway was opened, bringing tourists within seven miles of the Causeway. They could then complete their journey by jaunting car. Two hotels were built close by. One, the Causeway Hotel, offered hot and cold showers, 'Comfortable Cars with Careful Drivers always in Readiness, Good boats and Practical Boatmen.' The final piece in the jigsaw of access was the hydro-electric tramway, first of its kind in the world, linking Portrush and Bushmills in 1883. Although really intended to transport limestone and minerals, it was also to bring visitors *en masse* – in 1887, for instance, 62,000 came by the tramline, and the numbers continued to rise. Rush hour, when all the visitors wanted to leave at once, was a hair-raising experience.

When the National Trust took over the Giant's Causeway in 1961, one of its main tasks was to balance access to the stones with protection of the natural habitats from damage by the feet of visitors, currently running at over 500,000 each year. Dr Johnson's famous observation, that the Giant's Causeway is worth seeing, but not worth *going* to see, no longer holds true.

Wicken Fen: Britain's Rain Forest

Just seventeen miles north west of Cambridge lies Wicken Fen, 800 acres of undrained fenland, and one of the most important wetlands of Northern Europe. The names of its various components – Sedge, Adventurers', and Wicken Poor Fens – give the clues to its fascinating history.

Wicken, along with Chippenham and Wood Walton Fens, is all that remains of the Fens of the Great Level, over 2,500 square miles that once stretched from Lincolnshire to Suffolk. Around 4,500 years ago, the clay gault landscape experienced a series of inundations from the sea, building up layers of vegetation that developed into peat bog, and providing a challenge to the ingenuity of man. The Romans responded by creating canals through the fenland, such as Wicken Lode. In the Middle Ages the local population exploited the natural products, notably digging peat for fuel, and harvesting sedge for thatching, kindling and strewing. Saw Sedge, *Cladium mariscus*, lives up to its name; special leather gloves were used to handle it. Cut between March and August, it was transported by barge to Ely and Cambridge.

But peat and sedge seemed small fry to the agricultural entrepreneurs of seventeenth-century England. Spurred on by the drainage schemes of the Dutch, Charles I encouraged adventurers – speculators – to undertake similar schemes in what was significantly called 'the sink of the thirteen counties'. Francis Russell, 4th Earl of Bedford, agreed in 1630 to become the chief undertaker of a comprehensive scheme for the southern section of the East Anglian fens, gathering thirteen co-adventurers willing to risk capital in return for land once it was drained. With the help of a Dutch engineer, Cornelius Vermuyden, massive channels were built to carry water to the sea via the Great Ouse and the Nene. The rectangular pattern of these channels still dominates the East Anglian landscape.

At first the intention was to prevent summer flooding, but this plan was not completed by the outbreak of the Civil War. When Vermuyden resumed in 1649, his aim was to prevent year-round flooding. But what he failed to realise was that peat shrinks as it dries out, so that he and the adventurers of what was now called the

Albert Houghton (right), the Wicken bootmaker who set himself up as a professional ghillie, with his companion trapping moths at one of the 'Eddystone Lighthouses' at Wicken Fen, c.1894. (Royal Entomological Society)

Bedford Level Corporation were creating a problem for the landscape that is with us still, despite centuries of pumping to maintain levels of moisture.

The villagers of Wicken recognised that the draining was damaging and sought to halt the proceedings, first by riot and then by petition. The Bedford Level Corporation rejected their arguments and Adventurers' Fen was duly drained. But Sedge Fen and others remained, divided into strips on a common rights basis, and the villagers went on with their harvesting of sedge, peat digging and clay extraction through into the nineteenth century. Even when all the areas around succumbed to development, the people of Wicken held out, insisting that the natural fen products were more valuable than the arable crops produced on the drained land.

Their life was by no means easy. Ten acres of scrub and wet hollows known as Wicken Poor were divided into doles or shares in 1666 and set aside to provide peat and grazing for the poor of the parish. The domestic life of the fenlanders can be seen in Fen Cottage in Lode Lane, just by the entrance to the reserve. In the eighteenth and nineteenth centuries it represented two dwellings in the hamlet of The Lode. The owners were totally dependent on the fen for their food, their livelihood and the fabric of their houses. Fen Cottage has a chimney of brick from gault clay, walls of timber infilled with reed bundles overlaid with gault clay and lime daub, mixed with chopped sedge, and finished with lime plaster, and a roof thatched with sedge. Turf provided the fuel in the open hearth.

Despite the stubbornness of the fenlanders, it looked as if the traditional life and landscape at Wicken would finally have to change. Then help came from an unexpected source: the burgeoning study of entomology at Cambridge University. From the 1840s, drawn by the abundance and diversity of insect life, tutors brought their students out to Wicken, described as 'The Home of Ease for Entomologists'. Sedge cutters, knowing the value of the pupae of the Swallowtail, soon caught on, offering equipment, accommodation and expert guiding to the best spots. So many oil lamps were set up to attract the insects that complaints were made about Wicken looking like a city at night.

This lucky development ensured Wicken's survival. When yet another threat of draining loomed on the horizon in 1893, the entomologist J. C. Moberley bought up two acres of the commoners' strips and six years later sold them to the National Trust, then a very new organisation. The Fen was declared a nature reserve, the first of its kind in Britain. Visitors to Wicken can enjoy its very rich natural history. Successors to the Cambridge entomologists will see over 5,000 species of insect, including eighteen types of damsel- and dragon-flies. Butterflies include the Brimstone, Comma and Essex Skipper, flowers the Marsh Pea, Yellow Flag and Fen Violet. Hides have been built to observe a long list of birds from marsh harriers to bitterns and owls. Wicken's precarious past can be recalled by a visit to Fen Cottage and by inspecting the drainage windpump that continues to keep the water levels up and thus preserve this important wetland site.

Avebury: Millennium Dome

Avebury in Wiltshire is the most important Neolithic site in Britain, a complex of various monuments and earthworks which were used as a focus for ceremonial activities between 3700 and 2000 BC. It lies only twenty miles from Stonehenge, but in a very different landscape. While Stonehenge, with its great circle, stands isolated and bleak on a chalk plateau of the Salisbury Plain, Avebury is located at the headwater of the River Kennet, lying in much more fertile and welcoming surroundings.

The complex is indeed complex and bewildering to read from the ground. It includes: long barrows such as West Kennet; a causewayed enclosure of three ditches and a bank on Windmill Hill; stone circles and the remains of wooden ones on Overton Hill, 'the Sanctuary'; a huge earthwork rising from the valley floor at Silbury Hill; the stone circles, or henge, at Avebury itself; and an avenue of stones from this henge to the Sanctuary. All these features are associated with festivals, ceremonies and death scattered over a wide area, so that the modern visitor can only wonder at the industry that created them.

Attracted by the spiritual power of the site, and reassured by its fertility and closeness to good communication routes such as the ancient path of the Ridgeway, communities continued to inhabit the landscape around Avebury through the centuries – Iron Age forts, Roman villas, Anglo-Saxon earthworks with the Wans-dyke and, in the Middle Ages, a village and Benedictine priory established just outside the Avebury henge. At the Reformation a Tudor manor house took the place of the monastic community.

Although mentioned in passing by early topographical writers, Avebury's redis-covery as an historical site came a century later, when John Aubrey found the stones while out hunting with friends at Christmas 1648. As a Wiltshire-born man and an antiquarian, he was familiar with Stonehenge, but the stones and mighty bank at Avebury astounded him: indeed, he likened Stonehenge to a parish church, Avebury to a cathedral. He was to be fascinated by his 'cathedral' for the rest of his life, observing and drawing.

In 1662 Aubrey became a member of the newly-established Royal Society at the suggestion of his friend Walter Charleton, Royal Physician to Charles II. At a Soci-ety meeting on 12 July 1663 the two men presented their drawings of the stone circles at Avebury. Charleton was convinced that both Stonehenge and Avebury dated back to the Viking period and that one of the striking features of Avebury, the Tri-angle Stone, was a monument to a Danish king. Aubrey was the first to recognise, correctly, that Avebury was a prehistoric monument; his reading of Roman writers led him to believe that here was a temple of the Druids.

A month after the Royal Society meeting, Aubrey and Charleton accompanied the King and his brother, the Duke of York, on a visit to Avebury. After climbing up Silbury Hill, Charles II commanded Aubrey to 'digge at the bottom of the stones . . . to try if I could find any human bones: but I did not do it'. Instead, Aubrey undertook a detailed survey of the site, using a plane-table. The results were incorporated with his notes in *Monumenta Britannia*, a work still unpublished at his death in 1697.

The mantle of interpretation passed to William Stukeley. From 1723 he spent much time at Avebury drawing the monuments. Many of the stones had been broken up by villagers to build their houses. Like a war photographer, Stukeley realised that it was vital to record the site of each stone, even sketching an *auto-da-fé* with the destroyer extraordinary, Tom Robinson, burning straw in a pit to fragment the huge sarsens.

Stukeley had become convinced that Druid rites and symbolism were associated with Pythagorean harmonies and Egyptian hieroglyphics, and in particular with the symbol of a snake traversing a circle. The various monuments at Avebury, he decid-ed, formed an outline of a great serpent, with the monument he called the Sanctuary as its head, the Avenue its body, and its tail formed by the Beckhampton Avenue. As this theory developed, so Stukeley realised he was moving into dangerous

14

Labels in image: Rundway, ro. wad, Ro. Camp, Silbury, Windmill boll, Abury

territory as far as the Church was concerned. In 1729, therefore, he was ordained as a priest, announcing his intention to reconcile 'Plato and Moses, and the Druid and Christian religions'. His theories, with the invaluable and charming sketches of the monuments set in the landscape of Avebury, were published as *Abury: a Temple of the British Druids* in 1743.

Stukeley's work had put Avebury on the antiquarian map, but the debate as to its origins and use continued. Only archaeology could throw some light on the mystery. Aubrey had been ordered by Charles II to dig, but didn't. His contemporary, Dr Toope, discovered human bones at the Sanctuary and used them to make medicine for his 'distressed neighbours', causing Aubrey to comment: 'Toope was lately at the Golgotha again to supply a defect of medicine he had from hence.' Their successors made desultory efforts, but it was only in the early twentieth century that methodical archaeological investigation was begun. In 1908 Harold St George Gray from the Taunton Museum started work on the ditch at Avebury, moving down through the layers to prehistoric times. Not only did he show the immense depth of the ditch and the engineering skills of its makers, but proved at last that the chronology of Avebury stretched back over 5,000 years to the Neolithic, or New Stone Age.

William Stukeley's sketch of the Sanctuary made on 8 July 1723, shortly before much of it was destroyed. In the background can be seen the dramatic outline of Silbury Hill, with Windmill Hill and the village of Abury [Avebury]. (Alexander Keiller Museum)

In 1925 Gray was joined by Alexander Keiller. A rich man, inheriting a fortune based on marmalade, Keiller became involved with Avebury when Marconi threatened to build a wireless station on Windmill Hill. He removed the threat by purchasing the site, and continued to guarantee Avebury's protection by buying parts of the village and installing himself in the Tudor manor house. From 1934 to the outbreak of the war, he excavated the Kennet Avenue and the western part of the earthwork in Avebury, filling in some of the missing parts of the jigsaw. He was able to find many of the stones, buried in the Middle Ages by superstitious villagers, and re-erect them. He even found a medieval accident – the skeleton of a man who must have been killed by a stone in an attempt to fell it. The contents of his purse showed him to be an itinerant barber surgeon, living around 1320. This find, together with flints, bones and pottery, is in the Alexander Keiller Museum at Avebury.

In an article in the *Guardian* in July 1998, Jonathan Glancey likened Avebury to the Millennium Dome, with Avebury emerging very much the better from the comparison. What he liked about the monuments at Avebury was the fact that, despite all the work of the antiquarians and archaeologists, they remain a mystery to us. It was that mystery, too, that moved Aubrey to say that he had brought Avebury 'from an inner darkness to a thin mist'.

The Lake District: Through a Glass Darkly

The area of Cumbria and north Lancashire known as the Lake District is world famous for its picturesque scenery. Yet it is a surprisingly small area. During the Ice Ages, snow from domes of old, hard rock, now the peaks of Skiddaw, Helvellyn and Scafell Pike, pushed downwards, packing into icy glaciers that carved out the steep valleys, and melting into the deep waters that form the lakes. For centuries this dramatic landscape was remote and poor. In the Middle Ages great monasteries such as Fountains Abbey in Yorkshire kept their sheep in granges here, while some valleys were farmed by 'statesmen', independent families like the Brownes of Townend in Troutbeck.

The eighteenth century changed all this. When the rebel forces of Charles Stuart, the Young Pretender, managed to penetrate south as far as Derby, the government in London became alarmed by the lack of communication prevailing with Scotland. By 1768 the main route north through Westmorland and Cumberland was levelled and

surfaced. Where access led, taste followed. In October 1769 the poet Thomas Gray journeyed from Keswick to Lancaster, writing letters to his friend Thomas Wharton. With their publication, travellers made their way to the Lake District in increasing numbers, especially after the French Revolution and the Napoleonic Wars closed Europe to them.

Like Gray, many carried a Claude Glass in their baggage. This was a slightly convex mirror that enabled the viewer to create an image of the landscape imbued with the atmosphere of the painter Claude Lorraine. The cult of the Picturesque had taken hold. Its archpriest was the Rev. William Gilpin, Cumbrian born, who defined picturesque beauty as that kind of beauty which would 'look well in a picture', promoting his ideas through a series of books of tours. Landscape painters such as Francis Towne, John Constable and later Turner developed his ideas into pictures.

But Gilpin also suggested that it was not necessary for tourists to accept passively what they saw on their travels; rather they should develop their experience by using their imagination. This idea had already been taken up by Thomas West in his *Guide to the Lakes*. He recommended stations where the best views might be obtained. Claife Station overlooking Windermere is now a ruin, but in the late eighteenth century it was an octagonal tower with an upper room furnished with chairs, a fireplace, an Aeolian harp and three large windows, each bordered with coloured glass – yellow, blue, purple – so that the viewer could experience the cool of winter through to the mellow hues of autumn. This pastime was mocked in James Plumptre's play, *The Lakers*, in which the heroine looks across Derwentwater to Borrowdale, exclaiming, 'I must throw a gilpin tint over these magic scenes of beauty ... How gorgeously glowing! Now for the darker. How gloomily glaring! Now for the blue. How frigidly frozen!' She even considered employing it to view her lover.

Apart from Gilpin, all these interpreters of the landscape were visitors. But there was one native-born literary genius who stamped his mark indelibly on the Lake District. William Wordsworth was born in Cockermouth in 1770. While his father encouraged his literary interest by giving him access to his library and urging him to learn Shakespeare and Milton by heart, he also bequeathed him a straitened existence. John Wordsworth was legal and political agent to the 1st Earl of Lonsdale, a difficult, eccentric man who refused to pay William and his siblings the £8,000 owing at their father's death in 1783. His kinder heir finally paid up in 1802.

In 1799 William Wordsworth and his sister Dorothy set up home at Dove Cottage, just outside Grasmere. Many of William's finest poems were written here, including *The Prelude*, which recalled his childhood in Cockermouth, while Dorothy composed her journal. Thereafter they never left the Lakes, moving to Rydal in 1808 and attracting other literary figures such as Coleridge and Southey to join them. This group is often called the school of Lake Poets, but their literary style was disparate. What linked them was their interest in landscape and their appreciation of the local community. This interest was to inspire further generations of literary figures, including John Ruskin, who settled at Brantwood overlooking Coniston Water in 1872. Through his friendship with Hardwicke Rawnsley, vicar of Crosthwaite, his love of the landscape was passed to Beatrix Potter, while through his secretary, W. G. Collingwood, Arthur Ransome took up his ideas. Their books were to open up the Lake District to generations of children.

It would be a mistake to regard the Lakes as a pastoral idyll, untouched by industry. Quarrying, mining and smelting were traditional activities there since the earliest times. When Thomas Gray visited Sizergh in 1769, he saw not only the ancient castle, but also walked down by the river where he described 'the roar of the waters and the thumping of huge hammers at an iron-forge not far distant'. Water was then the major source of power and, had it remained so, problems that the remoteness of the area presented in establishing heavy industry might have been overcome. But this threat was removed by the development of steam and it was Lancashire and Yorkshire that became industrial centres.

Another threat took its place – the railways, and with them tourism and suburban development. In 1844 William Wordsworth led opposition to the railways progressing beyond Windermere, writing a sonnet for the occasion which asked, 'Is there no nook of English ground secure/From rash assault?' The answer was yes in this case. Forty years later Hardwicke Rawnsley was fighting a similar battle for Borrowdale, one of the most isolated valleys and one that had stimulated travellers to melodramatic heights. Ann Radcliffe wrote of it in 1794: 'Dark rocks yawn at its entrance, terrific as the wildness of a maniac.' In 1883 such thoughts of the sublime did not concern the railway developers but, like Wordsworth, Rawnsley won his battle. Borrowdale survived unscathed, and the Lake District Defence Society, and subsequently the National Trust, were founded to try to counter future threats of this kind. Today the Trust owns a quarter of the Lake District National Park, looking after the superb landscape for the benefit of thousands of visitors who flock there in the steps of the poets, painters and the seekers after the picturesque.

West Penwith – 'The World's Oldest Working Landscape'

The Cornish seaside town of St Ives is a picturesque place, even during the overcrowded summer season. It is this picturesqueness that attracted the sculptor Barbara Hepworth, her painter husband, Ben Nicholson, and their artist friends to set up their studios here in the 1940s. Drive westwards from St Ives, however, and you arrive in another country, a pagan landscape according to Hepworth, which gave form to many of her sculptures.

This is West Penwith, a rectangle of land stretching along the north coast down to Cape Cornwall and Lands End. To the one side the granite moorland rises to dramatic carns, on the other lie rocky headlands and coves, with farms surrounded by small, stone-hedged fields, narrow lanes, and here and there the remains of engine houses and chimneys. The countryside from St Ives to Pendeen is of intense and exquisite beauty; but it is also, according to local archaeologists, the oldest working landscape in the world.

At Rosemergy Farm, for instance, can be seen the form of an Iron Age farm. Three thousand years ago, when the climate was 2 or 3 degrees higher than now, Cornish farmers cleared small fields radiating out from their farmsteads, dividing them with Cornish hedges – walls of stone infilled with rubble and soil – and lynchets or terraces were formed to cope with the slope down to the sea. Here they grew barley and wheat, raised cattle and sheep, moving from field to field as the soil was exhausted. Forts were built on headlands such as Bosigran and Gurnard. Bosigran means 'farm of igran' and is said to be the home of Ygran, mother of King Arthur. Within the fort's defences there are no remains of a settlement, suggesting it might have been a meeting ground, neutral territory where trading could take place. Gurnard Head, on the other hand, has hut circles of stone, which would have carried timber central posts and furze roofs.

Iron Age huts gave way to Romano-Cornish houses, built around courtyards and strung along streets, and then to medieval farmsteads, as this land was constantly under cultivation. The sea, too, contributed to this precarious existence. From the late eighteenth century until the early 1900s, the main catch was pilchards. Vast shoals of them, flashing silver in the water, would cause all other activities to cease. A huer, stationed on the headland, would use a branch of gorse to signal to his companions in their seine boats, to indicate where the shoals lay beneath them. The catch was then packed into hogsheads on the shore, and loaded into sailing ships to go off to the Mediterranean countries, where pilchards were appreciated on days of abstinence from meat. The departure of the shoals was as dramatic as their arrivals – the industry died as a result of over-fishing.

The local name for pilchards was fair maids, probably a corruption of *fumadoe*, the Spanish for smoked. A very different maid, meanwhile, was involved in the third industry of this area, the mining of tin. In the eighteenth and nineteenth centuries, when the stone bearing the tin ore had been dug out, local women, known as bal-maidens, were employed to break the stones into fist-sized pieces. Places like Porthmoina and Porthmeor, now so tranquil, were seething with people, noise and machinery a century or so ago. At Porthmoina the original mining was surface, and the prospect pits can still be detected in the undergrowth. Later shafts were dug and the engine house erected for the winding gear. The stone came up to the spalling grounds for the attentions of the bal-maidens, before descending down wooden runners along a stream, with an overshot wheel providing the power for stamping machines to reduce further the size of the stones. Down again through a series of pools the tin ore descended to the beach, gradually being refined. Horses and carriages waited on the shore to take the ore eastwards to Hayle, where tin's faithful companion, arsenic, was burned off. At Porthmeor, a site that survived through to the diesel age, a burning house forms part of the complex. The deadly arsenic was then exported to the United States to kill off the boll-weevil preying on the cotton fields. Oddly close to the ruin of this burning house can still be seen the crows or sties where pigs were kept – a reminder of the close trinity of farming, fishing and mining.

Tincroft Mine, Illogan Parish, c.1900, with miners, bal-maidens and surface workers, known as 'grass captains' in white coats. (Royal Cornwall Museum)

Porthmeor and Porthmoina have now reverted to rural landscapes, the remains of the mining cloaked in undergrowth. Travel further westward to St Just and Cape Cornwall, and mining dominates the landscape. Scattered farmsteads give way to terraces of miners' cottages; engine houses and chimneys are everywhere. The great boom time in this part of the world was the second part of the nineteenth century, when St Just suddenly became a town. These mines were usually owned by co-operatives, financed by investors. At Botallack the Count House is being restored by the National Trust. On the ground floor were the administrative offices of the mine; above, a splendid banqueting room where the investors would be wined and dined. Close by is the Botallack Mine Set, including a magnificent building reminiscent of a Roman basilica. An arched flue ran like a snake through this building from the burning house to the chimney to provide the draw. To keep the draw effective, miners had to scrape the arsenic from the walls.

Reminders of the harshness of the miners' lives are constant. Many had to walk several miles to get to the pits, then climb down the shafts by ladder, sometimes to below the level of the sea, then walk another couple of miles to the face. Their traditional meal was a Cornish pasty – the filling was eaten, the pastry case thrown away because their hands were covered in arsenic. The average age of a Cornish miner in the late nineteenth century was twenty-seven. Even then, there was not enough employment, and thousands left to work in mines in Africa, America and Australia: it was said that you could shout down any hole in the ground in the world and a Cornishman would reply.

One such was Francis Oats, who began working at Botallack at the age of twelve, but emigrated to South Africa where he rose to become chairman of De Beers. On his return he bought Cape Cornwall, the most westerly point of England, building a fine house and landscaping the area. Within the valley at Cape Cornwall are the remains of each chapter in the whole history of mining. First came tin streaming, the method for extracting ore from Bronze Age times through to the Middle Ages. Then the Tudors mined both tin and copper by driving crude tunnels into the cliffs. Next came the surface mines and, after the inventions of Richard Trevithick, a local engineer, the mine shafts with their pumps and engine houses.

The last of the Penwith mines, Geevor, has just closed, bringing this long history to an end. The engines are still kept in working order at the National Trust's Levant Mine, but now Cornwall has perforce to replace the ancient trinity with a new one: farming, fishing and tourism.

Llanerchaeron: Mr Nash in Wales

Llanerchaeron lies on the very western seaboard of mainland Britain. A small country estate, it has been the home of ten generations of Welsh squires. The first of these was Llewelyn Parry, who bought 500 acres in the valley of the Aeron, close by the Cardigan coast, in 1634. Succeeding generations of Parrys, Lewis's and finally Lewes's farmed the lands around a medieval hall-house. Their estate was largely self-sufficient, with luxuries coming from Carmarthen and, on one occasion, China oranges and wine from a ship run aground. Llanerchaeron may be remote, but the family sent their sons to Oxford University, made careers in the Church and the law, and proved remarkably progressive in matters architectural.

By 1794 William Lewis had commissioned John Nash to remodel his house. Some ten years earlier, Nash had taken refuge in Carmarthen, his mother's native town, after financial disaster overtook his career as a speculative builder in London. Instead he established himself as a designer of country houses, producing a whole series of villas for his Welsh patrons. A fashionable concept of the time, the villa was entirely appropriate for Llanerchaeron: in ancient Rome and Renaissance Italy it was a working farm. For Lewis, Nash produced a compact house with an elegant Doric porch. Typical Nash touches included putting the servants' quarters to the side rather than in a basement: these were built in stone while the main house was in brick, to distinguish the rough vernacular from the polite.

At the very time that Nash was working on Llanerchaeron, a whole aesthetic debate on the picturesque landscape was being promoted by the publication of influential essays by Richard Payne Knight and his friend Sir Uvedale Price. Knight had based the idea for his house in Herefordshire on ruined medieval Welsh castles and set it in a landscape after the style of the painter Claude Lorraine. Price, for whom Nash had built a triangular Gothick house at Aberystwyth, proposed that buildings and land together should make a picture. In 1795 their theories were reinforced by a third publication, *Sketches and Hints on Landscape Gardening* by the designer Humphry Repton. He and Nash became partners, with Repton 'improving estates' while Nash provided the buildings.

We do not know who laid out the beautiful landscape that surrounds the house at Llanerchaeron, but it was certainly influenced by the idea of the picturesque. Within this landscape Nash not only designed the main house, but also an attached service court, a parish church in the style of a classical temple, and estate cottages in the rustic Gothick style that he was to make his hallmark. The home farm with its three yards was also either by him, or one of his followers. In 1796 Nash returned to England, gaining fame and fortune working for the Prince of Wales on his exotic pavilion at Brighton. He did not, however, forget William Lewis, and in 1820 designed for him the Assembly Rooms at Aberystwyth, the Brighton of Wales.

William Lewis was also a keenly progressive farmer, operating a sort of benevolent agricultural despotism. This obliged his tenants to lime their land and trim their hedges regularly, to bring their corn to his mill and rear a hound puppy apiece for his hunting kennels. But he also helped when rent was in arrears, or ex-servants needed his support. Wander around Llanerchaeron today, and his orderly spirit hovers. In the service court, so Italianate in feel, one range accommodates the dairy, cheese processing room and store, the range opposite contains the laundry and ancillary rooms, while a third, slightly later side holds the brewhouse and pickling larder. In the rick-yard of the home farm stand stone bases, one kind for drying hay, another for corn. One walled garden is for show, with heated walls to protect climbing plants, the second for kitchen produce, with a propagating yard behind with hotbeds and stoves, the gardeners' bothy and apple store. In the pleasure ground runs a picturesque stream, a leat from the ornamental pond to provide dipping wells for the gardens and water to sluice out the lavatories and drains. This ingenious combination of the aesthetic and the utilitarian runs right through Llanerchaeron.

Life continued little altered throughout the nineteenth century, when the estate was run by William's widowed daughter-in-law, Mary Ashby, who died at the remarkable age of 104 in 1917. When he moved in two years later the next squire, Thomas Ponsonby Lewes, ruefully observed 'everybody's aunt dies except mine'. The entire contents of the house, from the books in the library to the copper utensils in the kitchen, had to be auctioned to cover the debts of an earlier heir to the estate, while half the land was sold off to meet other commitments. It may have seemed a hard lot to Thomas, but it meant that Llanerchaeron survived as a superb, almost unique example of a Georgian country estate.

It was for this reason that the National Trust accepted the bequest of Llanerchaeron by Thomas's son John Powell Ponsonby Lewes at his death in 1989, even though there were insufficient funds to run the estate in the long term. Instead the Trust has embarked on a whole series of schemes that look to the future not only for Llanerchaeron, but also for the local community. These include the repair of the house and its ancillary buildings by local craftsmen, giving apprentices the opportunity to train in restoration skills. The home farm and parkland are being converted to organic status, with a flock of local Llanwenog sheep and organic field vegetables grown for sale to local co-operatives. Tenant farmers are being encouraged to use timber typical of the area, with a local yard to co-ordinate sales. The kitchen gardens bustle with life under the care of volunteers, who sell their fruit and vegetable crops to visitors.

Legacies are vital to help the Trust's work, but Pamela M. Ward's bequest was particularly welcome and timely. She left her collection of domestic chattels on condition that they be shown in a Georgian house. Llanerchaeron, bereft of its contents, fitted this stipulation perfectly. In addition, the Geler Jones collection of agricultural, domestic and craft bygones, acquired by the Trust in 1994, will be displayed alongside the artefacts that remain from the estate. In other words, Llanerchaeron is once more a living estate. Visitors are encouraged to see the work progressing, though the guidebook warns: 'You will not find here – yet – the familiar hallmarks of a National Trust property . . . hard hats are very much in evidence.'

Upper Wharfedale: A Priceless Legacy

When Graham Watson presented the National Trust with eight working farms in Upper Wharfedale, North Yorkshire, in 1989, his gesture was both generous and significant. For many years he would escape by motorbike with his brother David from their home in Bradford to walk in the Yorkshire Dales, and in 1943 they bought their first property in Upper Wharfedale, Beckermonds Farm. Gradually they bought others, building up an estate of 5,600 acres. David Watson's death in 1988 triggered Graham's decision to hand this estate over to the Trust while he could work with people whom he knew. Brushing aside plaudits, Graham explained that his gesture was 'not intended to be generous, it was selfish: we wanted to protect Upper Wharfedale and we knew of no other way of doing so'.

The Yorkshire Dales – dale is Viking for valley – were carved out of the Pennines by glaciers. As the rock is largely limestone, there are no lakes, but rivers and water-falls that tumble fiercely after rain, and reduce to a gentle trickle in dry seasons. On the uplands are the distinctive limestone pavements, grooved into fissures known as 'grykes'. Upper Wharfedale lies in the north western part of the Dales, running from Bolton Abbey up to Langstrothdale and providing a landscape of outstanding beauty.

For millennia this has been an agricultural landscape, with generations of farmers leaving their mark upon the countryside. At Grassington, when the sun casts long shadows, the ghostly forms of Iron Age field banks or lynchets come into focus. For Upper Wharfedale, the Dark Ages were probably not so dark: grazing and cropping were the order of the day rather than rape and pillage. By 866 Ivan the Boneless and his Danes had sailed up the Ouse and taken York. The Norwegians meanwhile crossed from Ireland and the Orkneys to Cumbria: the two groups meeting and integrating with the indigenous folk of the Dales. The rich mixture of place names reflects this: Wharfe itself is the name of a Celtic goddess, Hubberholme comes from the Old English for Hunburg's ham or homestead, while Yockenthwaite is the thwaite, Danish for clearing, of the Celt, Eogan.

This concept of rural integration was to be rudely shattered by the arrival of William the Conqueror, who put down a rebellion with ruthless efficiency and then extracted terrible revenge with a scorched earth policy known as the Harrying of the North. The survival of earlier names for settlements in Upper Wharfedale suggests that this area may have largely escaped the devastation, but the Dalesmen were now under the feudal government of William's leading supporters. Each peasant cultivated his strips scattered around the large arable fields, and remains of the characteristic ridge and furrow left by the medieval plough can still be seen in lynchet terraces known in the Dales as 'raines', and the inverted 's' in the line of drystone walls marks the turning of the plough. Some of the land, however, was set aside for the Norman passion for hunting. The chase of Langstrothdale was given to the Percy Earls of Northumberland, who maintained ten hunting lodges and housed their foresters at Buckden.

The third element in the medieval landscape of the Dales was the monastic granges. Following the harrying of the North, monasteries moved into the depopulated countryside and used the land to graze sheep. Gifts of land increased their holdings to such an extent that they came to own a quarter of the Dales, and prospered mightily. None more so than the Cistercian monks of Fountains Abbey who, by the thirteenth century, controlled lands as far west as Borrowdale in the Lake District, and sold 30,000lb of wool each year to merchants from Florence and Venice. Their headquarters in Wharfedale were at Kilnsey astride Mastiles Lane, the main route through to Cumbria. Here the manorial court met, the annual clipping and washing of sheep took place, and the fleeces were sent by wagon to Fountains Abbey.

Despite all their power and wealth, the great landowners and the monks were not to prove the enduring element here – late medieval politics and the Dissolution of the Monasteries put paid to them. Instead it was the small farmers who created the landscape that we see today, particularly in Upper Wharfedale, enclosing common lands with dry-stone walls. At first these enclosures were unofficial and usually irregular in shape, but the later 'parliamentary enclosures' are very regular, with walls as straight as a die swooping down the fellside. To improve the fertility of these upland areas, lime was burnt in kilns and scattered to counteract the natural leaching of the soil. In 1770 the agricultural improver, Arthur Young, reported how a farmer at

Greenfield Farm working at 1,200ft on the hillside 'intended to inclose and improve one field every year. The top vegetation is stripped off, then burnt, then limed. It was sown with turnips for two years, then laid down to grass. It turned out very profitable for pasture, milk cows, horses and sheep.'

Yockenthwaite provides a good example of a traditional Wharfedale farming community. A hamlet rather than a village, it is approached by a narrow packhorse bridge across the River Wharfe, and lies in the shelter of a belt of sycamores. At the end of the sixteenth century there were six farms; now there are only two, their farm-houses built in the eighteenth century with handsome Georgian doorcases and sash windows. Yockenthwaite Cottage still has the older, mullion windows.

In the fields around are the characteristic barns of the area, of local stone with lintels and copings of millstone grit. Cattle were overwintered on the lower level, in stalls separated by slate boskins, while a ceiling of woven hazel supported the hay in the level above. Traditionally the hay meadows were cut in July and the cattle allowed to graze until winter, when they were taken into the field barns. In spring the manure collected from the midden, a small enclosure adjacent to the barn, was spread onto the fields. The National Trust farms in Wharfedale continue this process of low intensity management, with farmers receiving grants to help to manage and maintain the unique landscape. The hay meadows are cut late to encourage wild flowers such as Yellow Rattle, Eyebright and Burnt Saxifrage.

Richard Muir in *Dales of Yorkshire* points out that 'the small farmer made the Yorkshire Dales, and when he goes, so too do the priceless vistas of meadows, pasture, wall and barn'. The future of many of the Dales farms is precarious because they are small hill farms trying to survive in an increasingly difficult environment. That is why the work of David and Graham Watson in buying and preserving the farms of Upper Wharfedale is so significant and valuable.

Corfe Castle and the Purbeck Coast: A King's Isle

The ruins of Corfe Castle are set dramatically on a steep hill with the village clinging around their base. It is a curiously un-English sight, much more like the *bastides* to be seen in the great valleys of southern France, the Lot, the Tarn and the Aveyron. Perhaps this is not entirely a conceit, for Corfe was one of the favourite castles of King John, who had an Angevin father and a mother from Aquitaine.

The castle stands on a mound that forms part of the main chalk ridge running east to west across the Isle of Purbeck, on the south Dorset coast. Two rivers cut through the ridge, creating the mound, and the name Corfe is derived from the Old English for a gap or cutting. The present castle was begun by William the Conqueror, quick to recognise the strategic value of such a site, though archaeological evidence suggests the presence of an Anglo-Saxon palace. Legend supports this, for Corfe is said to be the site of royal murder most foul – on 18 March 978, when Edward, King of Wessex and all England, was struck down by his stepmother, Elfrida, who wanted to put her own son Ethelred on the throne. Edward passed into history as the Martyr King, while his half-brother was dubbed Ethelred the Unready, and a Bad Thing according to *1066 and All That*.

But probably the greatest Bad Thing was King John. In 1204 he was forced to cede Normandy to his French cousin, making the south of England his vulnerable front line. Castles were strengthened along the coast, including Corfe, where his miners built a deep ditch between the castle and the village, and constructed fine new domestic quarters, known as Gloriette. The king's niece, the damsel of Brittany, was imprisoned here in some style and comfort, while her unfortunate knights were thrown into a dungeon called Butavant, and there starved to death. King John did nothing by halves. The castle survived intact until the Civil War in the seventeenth century, when it belonged to the Bankes family, loyal supporters of Charles I. While

Corfe Castle as a romantic ruin, a watercolour by J.M.W. Turner. (Victoria & Albert Museum)

Sir Ralph Bankes was in Oxford with the King, his indomitable wife, Brave Dame Mary, held off one Parliamentarian attack, but was forced through treachery to surrender the castle in 1646. Her bravery so impressed the Parliamentary commander that he allowed her to keep the keys of the castle, and these hang at Kingston Lacy, the fine house built by the Bankes at the Restoration. Corfe Castle was slighted to prevent it being used in war again, but so good was its medieval work that considerable remains survived.

From the castle fine views can be had over the landscape of the Isle of Purbeck; not an island at all, but a peninsula, roughly rectangular in shape, ten miles long by seven wide. It is quite geologically diverse, the layers running east to west like stripes in Neapolitan ice cream, and this diversity gives Purbeck a richness both of natural history and of landscape.

The most northerly part of the Isle is made up of a layer of grits and gravels yielding lowland heathland. In the Middle Ages this provided the hunting country so desired by the Norman and Angevin kings. King John made frequent visits to Corfe Castle so that he could hunt red deer and wild boar. To ensure that there was a good supply of these, Purbeck was declared a Royal Forest where Forest Law prevailed. The local populace was forbidden to grow hedges and build walls higher than could be jumped by a hind with a calf at her heel. Rangers and warreners prohibited the use of dogs, ferrets and nets. Islanders were not even allowed to marry their daughters to outsiders without official permission. Areas of heathland have survived at Studland, Godlington and Middlebere, but the red deer and the boar have gone. Instead all six British reptiles – Adders, Grass Snakes, Smooth Snakes, Common Lizard, Sand Lizard and Slow Worm – may be seen, along with the Dartford Warbler and the Northern Hobby.

The next layer is the chalk ridge on which Corfe Castle stands. Immediately south of the town is an area of fen and damp grassland which in earlier times served as its common land. Because it has never been ploughed, rich grassland flora such as Southern Marsh Orchid, Adder's Tongue Fern and Green-winged Orchid flourish. South again lies a valley of Wealden clay that has provided rich farmland for generations of settlers. At Peveril Point, for instance, the Celtic fields that have not fallen into the sea are still surrounded by their lynchets or terraces.

South again, the rock becomes limestone, with the landscape characterised by long dry-stone walls running north–south in parallel. These originally marked medieval manor boundaries, but today separate parishes and farms. This limestone ridge also yields the marbles of Purbeck and Portland stone. The latter was extracted right on the coast around Seacombe and St Aldhelm's Head, where the cliff quarries are supported by pillars giving them an architectural quality. In the seventeenth century this stone was dressed on shore and sent to London to rebuild the City churches and St Paul's Cathedral after the Great Fire of 1666.

Purbeck marble comes from two seams of hard limestone, one grey-green, the other red. It has been quarried since Roman times, but became internationally famous in the Middle Ages when the Crusaders returned from the Holy Land with a taste for marble. In this case the stone was not dressed at the quarries, or quarrs as they were known, but taken by hollow ways up to the village of Corfe Castle to be shaped by the masons and sculptors before being shipped from the port of Ower on Poole Harbour to various parts of England, Normandy and even Italy.

The architectural historian Nikolaus Pevsner noted that the first use of Purbeck marble in London was for the building of the Temple Church around 1160. The Templars were a military crusading order, founded to guard the Temple in Jerusalem, and their London church was one of the earliest conceived in the Gothic style in England. Others soon followed suit, so that Purbeck marble can be seen in some of the greatest cathedrals in the land: Canterbury, Winchester, Salisbury and Westminster. But it was the marble's use for tomb effigies that provided its international reputation. The fine workmanship of the Corfe Castle sculptors can be seen in the superb effigy of a bishop, perhaps Heraclius, patriarch of Jerusalem, in the choir of the Temple Church. The ultimate accolade, however, must be the effigy of King John in Worcester Cathedral, made in his favourite Isle of Purbeck.

Dunham Massey: The Benefit of Posterity

In the Great Gallery at Dunham Massey in Cheshire hang a series of remarkable pictures. Five are bird's-eye views of the house set in its gardens, parkland and estate: the first was painted in 1697 by Adriaen van Diest; the other four in about 1750 by John Harris. Another painting, by Jan Wyck and dating from the 1690s, is the most remarkable of all – the portrait of a Dutch mastiff called Old Vertue. On one side of him is the house at Dunham, on the other he is shown chasing sheep on the estate while a shepherd looks on – clearly he was an indulged pet. These pictures reflect what is special about Dunham Massey, an estate that remains remarkably intact and true to its eighteenth-century heyday.

Today the estate consists of 1,275 hectares, but if we go back to the Middle Ages it was much more extensive, stretching right up to Lancashire. A deer park surrounded the moated house, with agricultural land beyond and three townships, Dunham Town, Dunham Woodhouse and Little Bollington. In 1694 Dunham Massey was inherited by George Booth, 2nd Earl of Warrington. A cantankerous man, he quibbled over his father's will and quarrelled with his wife, Mary Oldbury, publishing a treatise on the desirability of divorce for incompatability of temper. But Mary was the daughter of a London merchant, and her £40,000 dowry provided Lord Warrington with the wherewithal to refurbish his estate. Perhaps it is significant that he chose to rebuild the existing Tudor house in plain Georgian style and to spend his money on the parkland around it. This seems to have been a recurring theme in a conservative family.

The alterations made to the estate can be seen by comparing van Diest's painting of 1697, when the work had just begun, with the Harris views, painted to celebrate the completion fifty years later. The former shows the house and formal gardens set within a park, with cattle, sheep and deer grazing. Various estate buildings can be identified, including the Mill, built in 1616 and still surviving. The later views show how the 2nd Earl laid out the Old Park in the formal geometric style pioneered by Le Nôtre, Louis XIV's gardener at Versailles. The whole plan is focussed on a *patte d'oie*, a goose foot, with a semi-circular line of trees at the convergence of six radiat-

George Booth, 2nd Earl of Warrington, the creator of the landscape at Dunham Massey. He is shown with his daughter and heir, Mary, in this portrait by Michael Dahl. (National Trust)

ing avenues of lime and oak. Between these avenues were blocks of planting, of oaks, elm and beech. According to *Hearts of Oak, the British Bulwark* published in 1763, Booth planted 100,000 trees, though more sober estimates set this down to 31,000 – still an enormous achievement.

The avenues radiated out into the estate so that, for instance, the Bollington Avenue continued over the meadows to the west, a *claire voir* in the park wall giving a view over the River Bollin to the open countryside beyond. Many of the park monuments set up as eye catchers have gone, but some remain, such as a deer barn, where animals could seek shelter and food in winter, and the slaughter house. The formal gardens were replaced by a parterre that could be enjoyed from the upper floors of the house. The 2nd Earl also created a walled kitchen garden, incorporating it into his grand landscape design, with a vista running east to west from a mound, which may have been the remains of a medieval motte and bailey castle, to a grand obelisk.

One witness to the unhappy marriage of the 2nd Earl and his Countess recorded that they 'lived in the same house as absolute strangers to each other at bed and board'. Despite this, they did produce one child, Mary, who married Harry Grey, 4th Earl of Stamford. The Greys were an old, distinguished family who counted among their forebears the tragic Nine-Day Queen, Lady Jane Grey. At Mary's death in 1772, Dunham Massey passed to her son, the 5th Earl, a cultivated man who no doubt found the style of the Old Park stiffly outdated. This was the time when Capability Brown and others were advocating a much more informal landscape style. However, the Booth trait of conservatism prevailed, and the 5th Earl contented himself with creating a New Park in an area of picturesquely undulating land to the north east, beyond the walls of the deer park, and merely loosened up the formality of his grandfather's work, allowing it to remain as a very rare example of early eighteenth-century landscape.

Beyond the walls of the park lay the estate, cultivated over the centuries by the tenants of first the Booths, then the Greys. In 1855 these farm tenants apparently refused to celebrate the marriage of the 7th Earl of Stamford to Catherine Cocks, daughter of a Norfolk gamekeeper, and a celebrated circus equestrienne. The Earl left Dunham, never to return. His successor, the 8th Earl, pursued an even more exotic private life in South Africa, marrying three times. His last marriage, to a Hottentot, was bigamous.

This period of absence came at a significant time for the estate. Agricultural depression was causing many of the old farm buildings to fall into disrepair. But Dunham no longer lay in isolated countryside: Manchester was rapidly developing just to the north. The trustees of the estate, recognising the potential of the metropolitan milk market, moved into a new phase of management. Old field boundaries, dating back centuries, were grubbed up, extra land was drained, farms enlarged and rationalised. Between 1900 and 1914 each farm was given a new farmhouse, pig cote, dairy, shippon and stable, built to a uniform design and painted in the estate livery of red, which still marks out the farms and estate buildings belonging to Dunham Massey.

In 1905 the Greys not only came back to Dunham, but also returned to the earlier style of careful estate management. Roger Grey, the 10th Earl, fought to preserve the landscape, preventing the Bollin Valley becoming a refuse tip and keeping electricity pylons out of the park, so that the estate that was given to the National Trust in 1976 represented a remarkable survival. Roger Grey is described in the Dunham Massey guidebook as dogged – a quality that would have appealed to his ancestor, George Booth, 2nd Earl of Warrington, who, when criticised by his friends for his extravagance in planting so many trees in his new landscape, replied: 'Gentlemen, you may think it strange that I do these things, but I have the inward satisfaction in my own breast; the benefit of posterity.'

Durham Coast: Turning the Tide

Most of the landscapes described in this diary have developed gradually over the years, centuries, millennia. But landscapes are very vulnerable, and can alter alarmingly quickly. Nowhere is this more evident than on the coast.

It was the threat of rampant development of Barmouth in North Wales as a seaside resort that impelled Fanny Talbot to donate Dinas Oleu, four and half acres of steep rocky hillside, to the National Trust in 1895, its first property. Building development on the coast is very difficult to reverse, but in other cases the process of regeneration is feasible and surprisingly swift in its effect. At Northey Island near Maldon in Essex, for instance, the salt marsh drained in the nineteenth century has been reinstated by the National Trust. By allowing the breaching of the sea wall that enclosed the drained land, a buffer has been provided to protect other areas vulnerable to flooding and to encourage the nature conservation of the area. Within only twenty months of the breaching of the wall, salt marsh plants had become established, a new creek was developing, and marsh birds were returning to the area.

Recognition of the vulnerability of Britain's coast came in 1965 when the National Trust launched Enterprise Neptune. Mrs Talbot's gift of Dinas Oleu had been followed by other donations and the Trust then owned 187 miles of unspoilt coast. Two years earlier a survey had been conducted to examine the overall situation of the 3,000 miles that make up the total coastline of England, Wales and Northern Ireland. Some areas were already protected by the Trust or other conservation bodies; of the rest, one third was deemed to have been developed beyond conservation, one third was considered of little interest, but one third was highlighted as being of outstanding natural beauty and worthy of preservation. Enterprise Neptune was created with the specific aim of acquiring this last, thousand miles – it is, in fact, the only area where the National Trust actively campaigns to acquire property. And it has proved very successful in this task: in the past thirty-five years, over £28 million has been raised and spent, and the Trust now protects a total of 590 miles of coast.

The halfway mark in Neptune's quest was a highly significant acquisition: the coal-blackened beach near Easington in County Durham, bought for £1 from British Coal in 1988. This coast, between the rivers Wear and Tees, has been supplying coal for British households and factories for centuries: for the past hundred years from collieries that stretched for miles under the sea itself. When J. B. Priestley visited the

The Vane-Tempest Colliery on the Durham coast, a photograph taken in the 1950s. (David Angus)

area in 1933 while compiling his *English Journey*, he likened the colliery town of Seaham to a 'carthorse with scales and fins'. Years of dumping the waste from the mines had covered the beaches with grime so that he found the towns even drearier than their inland counterparts, for 'the coast itself ... has a dirty and depressing look. The sea was dingy and had somehow lost its usual adventurous escaping quality.' To add insult to injury, the sea has also been heavily polluted with untreated sewage, causing one local MP to speak of 'not swimming, only going through the motions'.

Not a likely candidate for the attentions of the National Trust. But the Trust's director for this region in the 1980s, Oliver Maurice, was able to see the beautiful features that lurked under the grime, and to recognise the potential of this area once the collieries had closed, as inevitably they would. In 1987, therefore, he purchased Beacon Hill, a quarter of a mile of coast, from a local farmer. Three years later Hawthorn Dene was acquired. Denes are faults in the magnesian limestone which create wooded valleys. At Hawthorn Butterbur and Meadow Crane's-bill grow by the stream, Wild Garlic and Dog's Mercury in the woods of hawthorn, oak and ash. On the coastal clifftops the natural habitat is limestone grassland, home to flowers like Bloody Crane's-bill and the Rock-rose, and to the rare Durham Argus butterfly. Even the afflicted beaches represent important nature reserves, with different habitats within the width between high water and the cliffs. One conservator boldly claimed that Blast Beach, just south of Dawdon colliery and acquired by the Trust in 1990, was probably the most interesting it owns.

In 1933 J. B. Priestley pointed out ruefully that 'this part of Durham has done very well in its time for somebody, but not, somehow, for itself'. Now the Trust, with the support of local councils who had been battling for years to halt waste dumping, was determined to do something to provide a clean and attractive environment. Over the past decade the mines have indeed closed, enabling the Trust to purchase six miles of coast. The rubbish that inevitably accompanies industrial activities has been cleared, including two colliery heaps. Some of the clifftops that had been under arable cultivation are now returned to their natural habitat. But it is the sea that has displayed the most energy, removing 80 per cent of 40 million cubic metres of the spoil at a speed that has amazed. When Charlie Pye-Smith wrote *In Search of Neptune* to celebrate the Enterprise's twenty-fifth year in 1990, he hoped that 'black beaches would become golden': this hope is being fulfilled within an astonishingly short time.

The work continues, in conjunction with English Nature, the Countryside Commission and local authorities, with a millennium project, 'Turning the Tide'. With funding of £4.5 million, it is planned to create a place that is open and accessible, 'where people can enjoy the peace and natural beauty of the coastline'. Two more spoil heaps will be removed and the area laid down to limestone grassland. Within the coastal zone the emphasis is on walking, cycling, sea angling and public transport, including, it is hoped, new stations on the railway that runs along the coast but now stops only at Seaham. So, even Dr Beeching's tide might yet turn. And the horrid joke about the sewage-infested sea will be countered by Northumbrian Water's investment in sewage treatment plants and improved sea outfalls. The National Trust's pledge for its centenary was 'forever for everyone'. Here on the Durham coast, this pledge is being acted upon.

Sutton Hoo: A Place of Death

'Rime-crusted and ready to sail, a royal vessel with curved prow lay in harbour. They set their dear king amidships, close by the mast. A mass of treasure was brought there from distant parts. No ship, they say, was ever so well equipped with swords, corselets, weapons and armour.' These opening lines from the epic Anglo-Saxon poem, *Beowulf*, describe the mid-winter funeral of his father Scyld. A wonderful piece of poetry, but based on fact? Surely the arrival of the Angles and Saxons in Britain signalled the end of Roman civilisation and the beginning of the Dark Ages? It was the archaeological discoveries at Sutton Hoo that were to overturn these pieces of received wisdom.

Sutton Hoo lies beside the River Deben in Suffolk, up a slope of about 100 feet, on a terrace of turf broken by a series of grassy mounds. At the tip of the promontory stands Sutton Hoo House, built in the early part of the twentieth century. In the 1930s it belonged to Edith Pretty, a widow with a small son, Robert, and an interest in archaeology. She decided to find out what lay under the mysterious mounds and enlisted the help of a local archaeologist, Basil Brown.

Brown began digging into what became known as Mound 1 in 1938. As he investigated he realised that he was uncovering an Anglo-Saxon ship and, recognising its importance, experts were called in from the Office of Works and the British Museum. Their discoveries were spectacular. There were objects in gold, silver, bronze and iron, textiles, leather and wood, brought from all over the known world of the time, including Byzantine, Coptic, Scandinavian and Frankish work. The treasures were grouped as if in a burial chamber in the centre of the ship, but there was apparently no body – it was later discovered that the soil at Sutton Hoo acted like an acid bath. The ship itself was marked by rows of iron rivets, its ribs leaving strips of grey-black powder to provide the dusty ghost of a wooden, clinker-built vessel, 90 feet long.

In August 1939 the famous Anglo-Saxon scholar, H. M. Chadwick, came to look at the ship as it lay in the sand. He declared it to be the grave of Raedwald, King of the East Angles, who died *c.*625, an identification enormously exciting in its implications, for the Venerable Bede, writing in 731 in his *History of the English Church*, names Raedwald as the king who held sway over all provinces south of the River Humber. During a visit to Kent, he was converted to Christianity, but on his return to East Anglia his wife persuaded him to hold firm to his pagan loyalties. Like many faced with this dilemma, he probably kept his options open by placing in his 'temple' both pagan and Christian deities.

The archaeologists could now begin to look at the ship and its finds in their historical context. The lines from *Beowulf* describing Scyld's funeral began to echo through their heads, but so too did the threat of modern war. On 3 September 1939, the very day war was declared with Germany, the archaeologists stopped work on the site. Finding it impossible to refill the excavation trench on Mound 1, they covered the ship burial with bracken. Sutton Hoo became a training ground for the drivers of Sherman tanks, who found the undulations of the mounds particularly enjoyable for their manoeuvres until stopped by a discerning officer of high rank.

When the war was over, the treasures emerged from safekeeping in the London Underground and conservation work at the British Museum revealed them in all their beauty and sophistication. At Sutton Hoo, meanwhile, two further excavations took place, first in the 1960s when the ship burial was revisited and a broader exploration of the site took place under the supervision of Rupert Bruce-Mitford, and then again in the 1980s, when Martin Carver and his colleagues concentrated on the context of the cemetery and the origins of the kingdom of the East Angles. Although the site has never yielded up treasures of the richness found in the first mound, it has provided fascinating information about the culture and politics of seventh-century Anglo-Saxon England, and of its own development as a landscape.

For this is a landscape that has been exploited through the millennia. Originally it was heavily wooded with oak trees which were gradually cleared for agriculture, notably during the time of the Beaker People *c.*2000BC. Remains of their characteristic brown beakers and their circular huts were discovered under the Anglo-Saxon mounds. The acid soil of this area is easily exhausted, so that the Anglo-Saxons found above the river an open space where, in time, they erected eighteen mounds. The earliest, Mound 5, contained the cremated body of a youth who had been violently done to death. Other mounds covered the burials of skeletons, including one of a youth with the harness of his horse – the animal itself was buried nearby. The climax of the graves came with two ship burials.

In addition to these burials, which were clearly of high ranking people and undertaken with great ceremony, two groups of very different graves have emerged. The first was found close to Mound 5, the second to the east of the site. Most of the bodies showed evidence of garotting, beheading and dismemberment, while the second group seemed to be located around a wooden gallows. Carbon dating of these sad remains shows that the earliest was buried here in the seventh century, the last in the eleventh. Research has revealed that when the Anglo-Saxons united into one kingdom in the ninth and tenth centuries, a feature of royal authority was the

establishment of public killing at a *cwealmstow* or killing place. Could Sutton Hoo be the source of this concept, starting off with a vengeance killing for the violent death of the youth in Mound 5, and continuing through the centuries, even after the burial ground was abandoned and Christianity prevailed? The gibbet was finally moved to Wilford Bridge when the ferry route across the Deben was abandoned in favour of a road crossing. It remained there as a grim survival until the nineteenth century.

The National Trust has recently purchased the Sutton Hoo estate and plans to open the area containing the mounds to the public early in 2001. An interpretative exhibition will link this princely, ceremonial site with the everyday life of an Anglo-Saxon village at nearby West Stow, and with the magnificent ship burial finds in the British Museum.

The Anglo-Saxon ship under Mound 1 at Sutton Hoo, a photograph taken in 1939, during the later stages of excavation. (Trustees of the British Museum)

DECEMBER — JANUARY

27 MONDAY   BANK HOLIDAY (UK & EIRE)

28 TUESDAY   BANK HOLIDAY (UK & EIRE)

29 WEDNESDAY

30 THURSDAY

31 FRIDAY   NEW YEAR'S EVE
             BANK HOLIDAY (UK & EIRE)

1 SATURDAY   NEW YEAR'S DAY

2 SUNDAY

JANUARY

3 MONDAY BANK HOLIDAY (UK & EIRE)

4 TUESDAY BANK HOLIDAY (SCOTLAND)

5 WEDNESDAY

6 THURSDAY EPIPHANY

7 FRIDAY

8 SATURDAY

9 SUNDAY

South Foreland Lighthouse, Kent, built in 1843 to alert ships that they were approaching the notorious moving sandbank of the Goodwin Sands – 'the Great Ship Swallower'. The dawn of the new millennium is due here at 7.56am. (NTPL/Joe Cornish)

JANUARY

---

10 MONDAY

---

11 TUESDAY

---

12 WEDNESDAY

---

13 THURSDAY

---

14 FRIDAY

---

15 SATURDAY

---

16 SUNDAY

Langdon Cliffs at sunrise.
(NTPL/Joe Cornish)

JANUARY

17 MONDAY MARTIN LUTHER KING DAY (US)

18 TUESDAY

19 WEDNESDAY

20 THURSDAY

21 FRIDAY

22 SATURDAY

23 SUNDAY

*Many butterflies, including Chalkhill Blue (*Lysandra coridon*) seen here mating, are to be seen on Langdon Cliffs. (NTPL/Ian West)*

JANUARY

24 MONDAY

25 TUESDAY

26 WEDNESDAY

27 THURSDAY

28 FRIDAY

29 SATURDAY

30 SUNDAY

*On the beach at Langdon
Bay, with a wreck of one of
the many ships that have
come to grief in this area.
(NTPL/Joe Cornish)*

JANUARY — FEBRUARY

31 MONDAY

1 TUESDAY

2 WEDNESDAY

3 THURSDAY

4 FRIDAY

5 SATURDAY

6 SUNDAY

The beach at St Margaret's Bay, where the boulders cluster like huge sculptures at the foot of the chalk cliffs. (NTPL/Paul Wakefield)

❦ FEBRUARY

7 MONDAY

8 TUESDAY

9 WEDNESDAY

10 THURSDAY

11 FRIDAY

12 SATURDAY

13 SUNDAY

Detail from one of Susanna Drury's paintings in gouache on vellum of the Giant's Causeway, County Antrim, in the 1740s. Elegantly dressed gentlemen disport themselves amongst the basalt pillars. (The Trustees of the Ulster Museum)

❧ FEBRUARY

14 MONDAY ST VALENTINE'S DAY

15 TUESDAY

16 WEDNESDAY

17 THURSDAY

18 FRIDAY

19 SATURDAY

20 SUNDAY

Looking inland at the Giant's Causeway, with some of the hexagonal rocks in the foreground. (NTPL/Joe Cornish)

❧ FEBRUARY

21 MONDAY PRESIDENTS' DAY (US)

22 TUESDAY

23 WEDNESDAY

24 THURSDAY

25 FRIDAY

26 SATURDAY

27 SUNDAY

*Looking out seawards over
the Giant's Causeway.
(NTPL/Mike Williams)*

28 MONDAY

29 TUESDAY

1 WEDNESDAY ST DAVID'S DAY

2 THURSDAY

3 FRIDAY

4 SATURDAY

5 SUNDAY

A frosty day at Wicken Fen in Cambridgeshire. The windpump, the last of its kind, is now used to pump water from the Lode into the fen. (NTPL/Ray Hallett)

❦ MARCH

6 MONDAY

---

7 TUESDAY   SHROVE TUESDAY

---

8 WEDNESDAY   ASH WEDNESDAY (LENT BEGINS)

---

9 THURSDAY

---

10 FRIDAY

---

11 SATURDAY

---

12 SUNDAY   FIRST SUNDAY OF LENT

Harvesting Saw Sedge at
Wicken. (NTPL/Ray Hallett)

MARCH

13 MONDAY

14 TUESDAY

15 WEDNESDAY

16 THURSDAY

17 FRIDAY ST PATRICK'S DAY
BANK HOLIDAY (NORTHERN IRELAND & EIRE)

18 SATURDAY

19 SUNDAY

Lily pads on Drainer's Dyke, one of the seventeenth-century drainage channels that separates Sedge Fen from Verrall's Fen. (NTPL/Joe Cornish)

❦ MARCH

20 MONDAY

21 TUESDAY

22 WEDNESDAY

23 THURSDAY

24 FRIDAY

25 SATURDAY   ANNUNCIATION (LADY DAY)

26 SUNDAY   BRITISH SUMMER TIME BEGINS

Wicken Fen, Britain's first nature reserve, celebrated its centenary in 1999. This detail shows some of the flowers that can be seen, including Yellow Flag and Ragged Robin. (NTPL/Joe Cornish)

MARCH – APRIL

27 MONDAY

---

28 TUESDAY

---

29 WEDNESDAY

---

30 THURSDAY

---

31 FRIDAY

---

1 SATURDAY

---

2 SUNDAY FOURTH SUNDAY OF LENT
MOTHER'S DAY (UK)

Interior of Fen Cottage at Wicken, built in materials from the fen. This is the scullery, furnished as in the 1930s. (NTPL/Ray Hallett)

❧ APRIL

3 MONDAY

4 TUESDAY

5 WEDNESDAY

6 THURSDAY

7 FRIDAY

8 SATURDAY

9 SUNDAY

Dawn breaking over the stone circle at Avebury in Wiltshire. (NTPL/David Noton)

❧ APRIL

10 MONDAY

11 TUESDAY

12 WEDNESDAY

13 THURSDAY

14 FRIDAY

15 SATURDAY

16 SUNDAY   PALM SUNDAY

Aerial view of Avebury, showing how the prehistoric stone circle is enmeshed with the village. (NTPL/B.K.S. Surveys Ltd)

✿ APRIL

17 MONDAY

18 TUESDAY

19 WEDNESDAY

20 THURSDAY MAUNDY THURSDAY
FIRST DAY OF PASSOVER

21 FRIDAY GOOD FRIDAY
BANK HOLIDAY (UK & EIRE)

22 SATURDAY

23 SUNDAY EASTER SUNDAY
ST GEORGE'S DAY

*Avebury Manor, home of
Alexander Keiller while he
was excavating the various
prehistoric sites.
(NTPL/Oliver Benn)*

❦ APRIL

24 MONDAY EASTER MONDAY
BANK HOLIDAY (UK & EIRE, EXCEPT SCOTLAND)

25 TUESDAY

26 WEDNESDAY

27 THURSDAY

28 FRIDAY

29 SATURDAY

30 SUNDAY

A sarsen slab at Avebury,
with the great enclosing bank
and ditch behind.
(NTPL/David Noton)

☘ MAY

---

1 MONDAY <small>BANK HOLIDAY (UK & EIRE)</small>

---

2 TUESDAY

---

3 WEDNESDAY

---

4 THURSDAY

---

5 FRIDAY

---

6 SATURDAY

---

7 SUNDAY

A panorama of the Lake District taken from the summit of Catbells. To the right lies Derwentwater, to the left, Bassenthwaite Lake, with the peak of Skiddaw in the centre. (NTPL/Joe Cornish)

❧ MAY

8 MONDAY

9 TUESDAY

10 WEDNESDAY

11 THURSDAY

12 FRIDAY

13 SATURDAY

14 SUNDAY MOTHER'S DAY (US)

Derwentwater, viewed from Barrow Bay, with snow-capped Skiddaw and the spire of Keswick church peeping above the trees. (NTPL/Joe Cornish)

❧ MAY

15 MONDAY

16 TUESDAY

17 WEDNESDAY

18 THURSDAY

19 FRIDAY

20 SATURDAY

21 SUNDAY

Honister Pass in Borrowdale in winter. Little wonder that eighteenth-century travellers wrote of this valley in terms of terror and awe. (NTPL/Joe Cornish)

MAY

22 MONDAY

23 TUESDAY

24 WEDNESDAY

25 THURSDAY

26 FRIDAY

27 SATURDAY

28 SUNDAY

Lodore Falls on the shores of Derwentwater, painted by Francis Towne in 1786. Dr John Dalton wrote of the falls in 1755 'Horrors like these at first alarm/But soon with savage grandeur charm'. Keats later complained about the lack of water, while Southey wrote a doggerel poem in 1820 imitating the shape of the water and its sound. (Christies Images)

29 MONDAY BANK HOLIDAY (UK)
MEMORIAL DAY (US)

30 TUESDAY

31 WEDNESDAY

1 THURSDAY ASCENSION DAY

2 FRIDAY

3 SATURDAY

4 SUNDAY SUNDAY AFTER ASCENSION

Dawn over Derwentwater.
(NTPL/David Noton)

JUNE

5 MONDAY   BANK HOLIDAY (EIRE)

---

6 TUESDAY

---

7 WEDNESDAY

---

8 THURSDAY

---

9 FRIDAY

---

10 SATURDAY

---

11 SUNDAY   WHIT SUNDAY (PENTECOST)

The ancient landscape of West Penwith in Cornwall, the fields divided by stone hedges. (NTPL/Joe Cornish)

🌿 JUNE

---

12 MONDAY

---

13 TUESDAY

---

14 WEDNESDAY

---

15 THURSDAY

---

16 FRIDAY

---

17 SATURDAY

---

18 SUNDAY   TRINITY SUNDAY
FATHER'S DAY (UK & US)

Looking down from Carn Galver to Bosigran and the north Cornish coast. (NTPL/Joe Cornish)

JUNE

19 MONDAY

20 TUESDAY

21 WEDNESDAY

22 THURSDAY

23 FRIDAY

24 SATURDAY   MIDSUMMER'S DAY – THE LONGEST DAY

25 SUNDAY

The mouth of the Kenidjack Valley at St Just, with the remains of Wheal Call wheelpit on the right, and the pumping engine house for the tin mine in the distance. (NTPL/Graeme Norways)

26 MONDAY

27 TUESDAY

28 WEDNESDAY

29 THURSDAY

30 FRIDAY

1 SATURDAY

2 SUNDAY

Cape Cornwall, England's only cape and its most westerly point. (NTPL/Joe Cornish)

❦ JULY

3 MONDAY

---

4 TUESDAY INDEPENDENCE DAY (US)

---

5 WEDNESDAY

---

6 THURSDAY

---

7 FRIDAY

---

8 SATURDAY

---

9 SUNDAY

Llanerchaeron estate in Dyfed, with John Nash's Georgian villa nestling in the wooded valley of the Aeron. (NTPL/Chris King)

JULY

10 MONDAY

11 TUESDAY

12 WEDNESDAY BANK HOLIDAY (NORTHERN IRELAND)

13 THURSDAY

14 FRIDAY

15 SATURDAY

16 SUNDAY

A tip cart in the stable yard, with a fine example of a pitched stone floor laid out in a herringbone pattern. (NTPL/Chris King)

JULY

17 MONDAY

18 TUESDAY

19 WEDNESDAY

20 THURSDAY

21 FRIDAY

22 SATURDAY

23 SUNDAY

A window in one of the outhouses in the stable yard. (NTPL/Chris King)

❧ JULY

24 MONDAY

25 TUESDAY

26 WEDNESDAY

27 THURSDAY

28 FRIDAY

29 SATURDAY

30 SUNDAY

Stone masons using traditional lime mortar to repair the rear wall of the cattle sheds at the home farm at Llanerchaeron. (NTPL/Chris King)

❦ SEPTEMBER

---

11 MONDAY

---

12 TUESDAY

---

13 WEDNESDAY

---

14 THURSDAY

---

15 FRIDAY

---

16 SATURDAY

---

17 SUNDAY

*A Sand Lizard on a wooden
stump on Dorset heathland.
(NTPL/Jim Hallett)*

AUGUST

7 MONDAY BANK HOLIDAY (SCOTLAND & EIRE)

8 TUESDAY

9 WEDNESDAY

10 THURSDAY

11 FRIDAY

12 SATURDAY

13 SUNDAY

The great cellarium at Fountains Abbey, where the fleeces – the source of the monastery's wealth – were stored in the Middle Ages. (NTPL/Geoff Morgan)

❦ AUGUST

14 MONDAY

15 TUESDAY

16 WEDNESDAY

17 THURSDAY

18 FRIDAY

19 SATURDAY

20 SUNDAY

*Chris Alkrigg, the tenant
farmer, with one of his
Swaledales at Manor Farm,
Upper Wharfedale.
(NTPL/Michael Caldwell)*

❧ AUGUST

21 MONDAY

22 TUESDAY

23 WEDNESDAY

24 THURSDAY

25 FRIDAY

26 SATURDAY

27 SUNDAY

The landscape at Scarhouse, with a typical field barn in the foreground.
(NTPL/Michael Caldwell)

28 MONDAY <small>BANK HOLIDAY (UK, EXCEPT SCOTLAND)</small>

29 TUESDAY

30 WEDNESDAY

31 THURSDAY

1 FRIDAY

2 SATURDAY

3 SUNDAY

Looking down on the hamlet
of Yockenthwaite.
(NTPL/Joe Cornish)

❧ SEPTEMBER

4 MONDAY LABOR DAY (US)

5 TUESDAY

6 WEDNESDAY

7 THURSDAY

8 FRIDAY

9 SATURDAY

10 SUNDAY

The ruins of Corfe Castle in Dorset, silhouetted against the setting sun. (NTPL/David Sellman)

SEPTEMBER

11 MONDAY

12 TUESDAY

13 WEDNESDAY

14 THURSDAY

15 FRIDAY

16 SATURDAY

17 SUNDAY

A Sand Lizard on a wooden stump on Dorset heathland. (NTPL/Jim Hallett)

❦ SEPTEMBER

18 MONDAY

19 TUESDAY

20 WEDNESDAY

21 THURSDAY

22 FRIDAY

23 SATURDAY

24 SUNDAY

St Aldhelm's Head on the most southerly tip of the Isle of Purbeck. This is a highly worked landscape: Purbeck limestone has been quarried for centuries for cathedrals and palaces. (NTPL/Joe Cornish)

25 MONDAY

26 TUESDAY

27 WEDNESDAY

28 THURSDAY

29 FRIDAY MICHAELMAS DAY

30 SATURDAY ROSH HASHANAH

1 SUNDAY

The chalk cliffs of Ballard Point on the eastern shore of the Isle of Purbeck. (NTPL/David Noton)

❧ OCTOBER

2 MONDAY

3 TUESDAY

4 WEDNESDAY

5 THURSDAY

6 FRIDAY

7 SATURDAY

8 SUNDAY

Fallow Deer in the deer park at Dunham Massey in Cheshire. (NTPL/Nick Meers)

❧ OCTOBER

9 MONDAY COLUMBUS DAY (US)
YOM KIPPUR

10 TUESDAY

11 WEDNESDAY

12 THURSDAY

13 FRIDAY

14 SATURDAY

15 SUNDAY

*The Mill at Dunham Massey.
Built in 1616, it survived the
eighteenth-century
remodelling of the estate by
George Booth, 2nd Earl of
Warrington.
(NTPL/Matthew Antrobus)*

❧ OCTOBER

16 MONDAY

17 TUESDAY

18 WEDNESDAY

19 THURSDAY

20 FRIDAY

21 SATURDAY

22 SUNDAY

Adriaen van Diest's bird's-eye view of Dunham Massey, painted in 1697, showing the Tudor house, formal gardens and surrounding estate before the changes made by Lord Warrington. (NTPL/Angelo Hornak)

❦ OCTOBER

23 MONDAY

24 TUESDAY

25 WEDNESDAY

26 THURSDAY

27 FRIDAY

28 SATURDAY

29 SUNDAY BRITISH SUMMER TIME ENDS

John Harris's bird's-eye view of Dunham Massey from the north, painted in 1750 when the remodelling was complete. The house has been rebuilt in a plain Georgian style, but the dramatic change lies in the layout of the gardens and park, including a great patte-d'oie or goose-foot, with avenues of lime, beech and oak radiating out into the estate. (NTPL/Angelo Hornak)

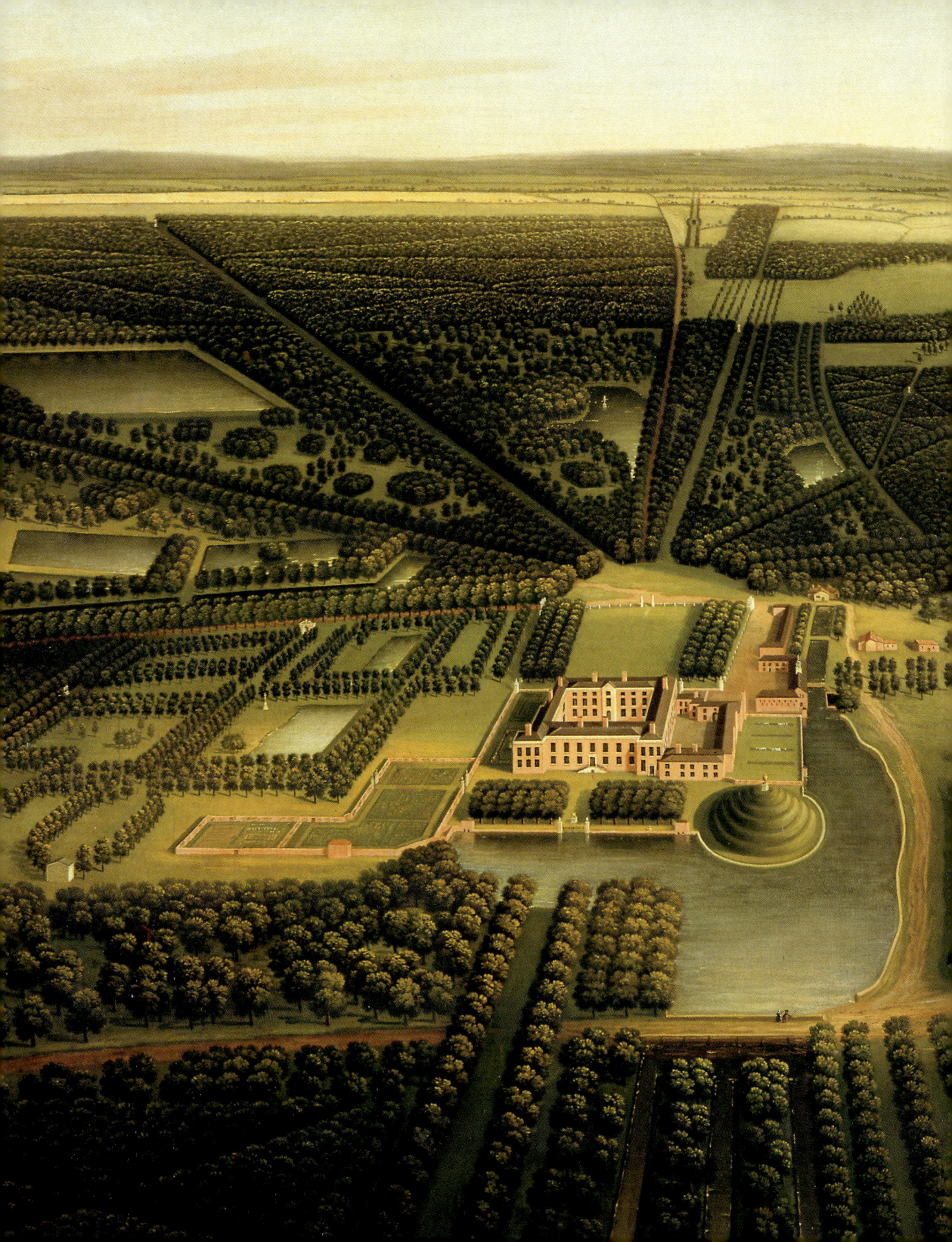

OCTOBER – NOVEMBER

30 MONDAY BANK HOLIDAY (EIRE)

31 TUESDAY HALLOWE'EN

1 WEDNESDAY ALL SAINTS' DAY

2 THURSDAY

3 FRIDAY

4 SATURDAY

5 SUNDAY GUY FAWKES' NIGHT

Northey Island, near Maldon in Essex. This photograph was taken twenty months after the sea wall had been breached, and shows marsh plants growing to the side of the new creek. (NTPL/Joe Cornish)

🌿 NOVEMBER

---

6 MONDAY

---

7 TUESDAY

---

8 WEDNESDAY

---

9 THURSDAY

---

10 FRIDAY

---

11 SATURDAY VETERANS' DAY (US)

---

12 SUNDAY REMEMBRANCE SUNDAY

The coal-blackened beach below Easington Colliery on the north Durham coast. This photograph was taken in 1989, shortly after the Trust bought it from British Coal for £1. In the decade since, the sea has gradually removed much of the spoil that had been dumped from the mines. (NTPL/Joe Cornish)

❧ NOVEMBER

13 MONDAY

14 TUESDAY

15 WEDNESDAY

16 THURSDAY

17 FRIDAY

18 SATURDAY

19 SUNDAY

Hawthorn Dene, looking over to Chourdon Point, with the railway that runs along the coast. Since this photograph was taken in 1989 the land has been returned from arable cultivation to limestone grassland to encourage the rich natural flora. (NTPL/Joe Cornish)

❧ NOVEMBER

20 MONDAY

21 TUESDAY

22 WEDNESDAY

23 THURSDAY THANKSGIVING DAY (US)

24 FRIDAY

25 SATURDAY

26 SUNDAY

Bloody Crane's-bill, one of the wild flowers that flourishes on limestone grassland. (NTPL/Joe Cornish)

27 MONDAY

28 TUESDAY

29 WEDNESDAY

30 THURSDAY ST ANDREW'S DAY

1 FRIDAY

2 SATURDAY

3 SUNDAY FIRST SUNDAY IN ADVENT

Looking across the Anglo-Saxon burial mounds at Sutton Hoo in Suffolk on a frosty morning. (NTPL/Joe Cornish)

❦ DECEMBER

4 MONDAY

5 TUESDAY

6 WEDNESDAY

7 THURSDAY

8 FRIDAY

9 SATURDAY

10 SUNDAY

The spectacular seventh-century helmet found in the ship burial in Mound 1 at Sutton Hoo. (Trustees of the British Museum)

❦ DECEMBER

---

11 MONDAY

---

12 TUESDAY

---

13 WEDNESDAY

---

14 THURSDAY

---

15 FRIDAY

---

16 SATURDAY

---

17 SUNDAY

Detail of the 'sceptre' from Mound 1. This shows the delicately modelled bronze stag and part of the massive whetstone. The precise function of this object is still not fully understood. (Trustees of the British Museum)

DECEMBER

18 MONDAY

19 TUESDAY

20 WEDNESDAY

21 THURSDAY THE SHORTEST DAY

22 FRIDAY HANUKKAH

23 SATURDAY

24 SUNDAY CHRISTMAS EVE

A purse-lid from the ship burial. The gold frame is set with garnets and glass, and contains a modern lid with plaques in gold, garnet and millefiori. (Trustees of the British Museum)

❦ DECEMBER

---

25 MONDAY CHRISTMAS DAY
BANK HOLIDAY (UK & EIRE)

---

26 TUESDAY BOXING DAY
BANK HOLIDAY (UK & EIRE)

---

27 WEDNESDAY

---

28 THURSDAY

---

29 FRIDAY

---

30 SATURDAY

---

31 SUNDAY NEW YEAR'S EVE

Frosted leaves at Sutton Hoo.
(NTPL/Joe Cornish)

1999

	JANUARY	FEBRUARY	MARCH	APRIL	MAY	JUNE
Monday	4 11 18 25	1 8 15 22	1 8 15 22 29	5 12 19 26	3 10 17 24 31	7 14 21 28
Tuesday	5 12 19 26	2 9 16 23	2 9 16 23 30	6 13 20 27	4 11 18 25	1 8 15 22 29
Wednesday	6 13 20 27	3 10 17 24	3 10 17 24 31	7 14 21 28	5 12 19 26	2 9 16 23 30
Thursday	7 14 21 28	4 11 18 25	4 11 18 25	1 8 15 22 29	6 13 20 27	3 10 17 24
Friday	1 8 15 22 29	5 12 19 26	5 12 19 26	2 9 16 23 30	7 14 21 28	4 11 18 25
Saturday	2 9 16 23 30	6 13 20 27	6 13 20 27	3 10 17 24	1 8 15 22 29	5 12 19 26
Sunday	3 10 17 24 31	7 14 21 28	7 14 21 28	4 11 18 25	2 9 16 23 30	6 13 20 27

	JULY	AUGUST	SEPTEMBER	OCTOBER	NOVEMBER	DECEMBER
Monday	5 12 19 26	2 9 16 23 30	6 13 20 27	4 11 18 25	1 8 15 22 29	6 13 20 27
Tuesday	6 13 20 27	3 10 17 24 31	7 14 21 28	5 12 19 26	2 9 16 23 30	7 14 21 28
Wednesday	7 14 21 28	4 11 18 25	1 8 15 22 29	6 13 20 27	3 10 17 24	1 8 15 22 29
Thursday	1 8 15 22 29	5 12 19 26	2 9 16 23 30	7 14 21 28	4 11 18 25	2 9 16 23 30
Friday	2 9 16 23 30	6 13 20 27	3 10 17 24	1 8 15 22 29	5 12 19 26	3 10 17 24 31
Saturday	3 10 17 24 31	7 14 21 28	4 11 18 25	2 9 16 23 30	6 13 20 27	4 11 18 25
Sunday	4 11 18 25	1 8 15 22 29	5 12 19 26	3 10 17 24 31	7 14 21 28	5 12 19 26

2000

	JANUARY	FEBRUARY	MARCH	APRIL	MAY	JUNE
Monday	3 10 17 24 31	7 14 21 28	6 13 20 27	3 10 17 24	1 8 15 22 29	5 12 19 26
Tuesday	4 11 18 25	1 8 15 22 29	7 14 21 28	4 11 18 25	2 9 16 23 30	6 13 20 27
Wednesday	5 12 19 26	2 9 16 23	1 8 15 22 29	5 12 19 26	3 10 17 24 31	7 14 21 28
Thursday	6 13 20 27	3 10 17 24	2 9 16 23 30	6 13 20 27	4 11 18 25	1 8 15 22 29
Friday	7 14 21 28	4 11 18 25	3 10 17 24 31	7 14 21 28	5 12 19 26	2 9 16 23 30
Saturday	1 8 15 22 29	5 12 19 26	4 11 18 25	1 8 15 22 29	6 13 20 27	3 10 17 24
Sunday	2 9 16 23 30	6 13 20 27	5 12 19 26	2 9 16 23 30	7 14 21 28	4 11 18 25

	JULY	AUGUST	SEPTEMBER	OCTOBER	NOVEMBER	DECEMBER
Monday	3 10 17 24 31	7 14 21 28	4 11 18 25	2 9 16 23 30	6 13 20 27	4 11 18 25
Tuesday	4 11 18 25	1 8 15 22 29	5 12 19 26	3 10 17 24 31	7 14 21 28	5 12 19 26
Wednesday	5 12 19 26	2 9 16 23 30	6 13 20 27	4 11 18 25	1 8 15 22 29	6 13 20 27
Thursday	6 13 20 27	3 10 17 24 31	7 14 21 28	5 12 19 26	2 9 16 23 30	7 14 21 28
Friday	7 14 21 28	4 11 18 25	1 8 15 22 29	6 13 20 27	3 10 17 24	1 8 15 22 29
Saturday	1 8 15 22 29	5 12 19 26	2 9 16 23 30	7 14 21 28	4 11 18 25	2 9 16 23 30
Sunday	2 9 16 23 30	6 13 20 27	3 10 17 24	1 8 15 22 29	5 12 19 26	3 10 17 24 31

2001

	JANUARY	FEBRUARY	MARCH	APRIL	MAY	JUNE
Monday	1 8 15 22 29	5 12 19 26	5 12 19 26	2 9 16 23 30	7 14 21 28	4 11 18 25
Tuesday	2 9 16 23 30	6 13 20 27	6 13 20 27	3 10 17 24	1 8 15 22 29	5 12 19 26
Wednesday	3 10 17 24 31	7 14 21 28	7 14 21 28	4 11 18 25	2 9 16 23 30	6 13 20 27
Thursday	4 11 18 25	1 8 15 22	1 8 15 22 29	5 12 19 26	3 10 17 24 31	7 14 21 28
Friday	5 12 19 26	2 9 16 23	2 9 16 23 30	6 13 20 27	4 11 18 25	1 8 15 22 29
Saturday	6 13 20 27	3 10 17 24	3 10 17 24 31	7 14 21 28	5 12 19 26	2 9 16 23 30
Sunday	7 14 21 28	4 11 18 25	4 11 18 25	1 8 15 22 29	6 13 20 27	3 10 17 24

	JULY	AUGUST	SEPTEMBER	OCTOBER	NOVEMBER	DECEMBER
Monday	2 9 16 23 30	6 13 20 27	3 10 17 24	1 8 15 22 29	5 12 19 26	3 10 17 24 31
Tuesday	3 10 17 24 31	7 14 21 28	4 11 18 25	2 9 16 23 30	6 13 20 27	4 11 18 25
Wednesday	4 11 18 25	1 8 15 22 29	5 12 19 26	3 10 17 24 31	7 14 21 28	5 12 19 26
Thursday	5 12 19 26	2 9 16 23 30	6 13 20 27	4 11 18 25	1 8 15 22 29	6 13 20 27
Friday	6 13 20 27	3 10 17 24 31	7 14 21 28	5 12 19 26	2 9 16 23 30	7 14 21 28
Saturday	7 14 21 28	4 11 18 25	1 8 15 22 29	6 13 20 27	3 10 17 24	1 8 15 22 29
Sunday	1 8 15 22 29	5 12 19 26	2 9 16 23 30	7 14 21 28	4 11 18 25	2 9 16 23 30